AAT Certificate in Accounting
Level 2
The Business Environment

First edition 2021

ISBN 9781 5097 4272 1

eISBN 9781 5097 4246 2

British Library Cataloguing-in-Publication Data

A catalogue record for this book is available from the

Published by

BPP Learning Media Ltd,
BPP House, Aldine Place,
142–144 Uxbridge Road,
London W12 8AA

www.bpp.com/learningmedia

Printed in the United Kingdom

British Library

Welcome to BPP Learning Media's AAT **Passcards** for **The Business Environment.**

- They **save you time**. Important topics are summarised for you.
- They incorporate **diagrams** to kick start your memory.
- They follow the overall **structure** of the BPP Course Books, but BPP's AAT **Passcards** are not just a condensed book. Each card has been separately designed for clear presentation. Topics are self-contained and can be grasped visually.
- AAT **Passcards** are still **just the right size** for pockets and bags.
- AAT **Passcards focus on the assessment** you will be facing.
- AAT **Passcards focus on the essential points** that you need to know in the workplace, or when completing your assessment.

Run through the complete set of **Passcards** as often as you can during your final revision period. The day before the assessment, try to go through the **Passcards** again! You will then be well on your way to completing the assessment successfully.

Good luck!

For reference to the Bibliography of the AAT The Business Environment Passcards please go to www.bpp.com/learning-media/about/bibliographies

Page

1	Principles of contract law	1
2	The external business environment	15
3	Principles of corporate social responsibility (CSR), ethics and sustainability	23
4	Business entities	37
5	The finance function	51
6	Working effectively	63
7	Importance of information	83

The BPP **Question Bank** contains activities and assessments that provide invaluable practice in the skills you need to complete this unit successfully.

1: Principles of contract law

Topic List

Classifications of law

Main sources of law

Key features of contracts

Remedies for breach of contract

Contract law is one element of law that forms part of the business environment. For businesses to have a degree of certainty in their operations, it is important for them to be able to trust that the agreements they make with other organisations can be relied upon.

A contract is a legally enforceable agreement which means that if one party fails to perform their agreed obligations (such as to deliver or pay for a product) then the other party has some certainty in knowing what the consequences will be, for example they will be paid compensation for any losses caused.

What is law?

Law is the enforceable body of rules that govern any society.

Types of law

Common law and equity

Common law is judge-made law which is developed by amalgamating local customary laws into one 'law of the land'. Remedies are monetary.

Equity was brought in to introduce fairness into the legal system and offers alternative remedies when money is not sufficient.

Statute law

This is law **created by Parliament** in the form of statutes.

Statute law is usually made in areas so complicated or unique that common law alternatives are unlikely or would take too long to develop.

Private law and public law

Private law deals with relationships between private individuals, groups or organisations.

The state provides the legal framework (such as statutes) that allows individuals to handle the matters themselves. The state does not get involved.

Public law is concerned with government and the functions of public organisations.

The key difference between public and private law is that it is the **state** that **prosecutes** under **public law** whereas the individual takes up the action in private law.

Criminal law and criminal liability

A **crime** is conduct prohibited by law. Crimes are punishable, usually by fine or imprisonment.

The state prosecutes. It must prove **beyond reasonable doubt** that the accused committed the crime.

Civil law and civil liability

Civil law exist to regulate disputes over the rights and obligations of persons dealing with each other.

The claimant must prove on **balance of probabilities** that the defendant caused the damage. A key area for businesses is **contract**.

The distinction is not the act but the legal consequences.

Courts

Courts create common law when they make decisions on a case heard before them. Decisions of future courts are expected to be consistent with previous cases. This is the basis of the system of **judicial precedent.**

Judicial precedent

The idea of judicial precedent means that **a judge is bound to apply a decision** from an earlier case to the facts of the case before them, provided there is **no material difference** between the cases and the previous case created a 'binding' precedent.

Tracking system

Civil cases are allocated to one of three tracks depending on their size and complexity.

Small claims track – value under £10,000

Fast track – value between £10,000 and £25,000 and take a day of court time

Multi-track – value over £25,000 and complex cases

Hierarchy of civil law courts
Supreme Court Final appeal court
Court of Appeal Hears appeals from lower courts
High Court Multi-track – for complex cases Claims over £25,000
County Court Fast-track – one day cases Claims between £10,000 and £25,000
County Court Small claims track Claims less than £10,000

Hierarchy of criminal law courts
Supreme Court Final appeal court
Court of Appeal Hears appeals from Crown Courts.
High Court Hears some appeals from Magistrate's and Crown Courts.
Crown Court Tries major offences and hears appeals from Magistrate's Courts for minor offences.
Magistrate's Court Tries minor offences, passes major offences to the Crown Court.

Classifications of law	Main sources of law	Key features of contracts	Remedies for breach of contract

Tribunals

Tribunals are a **slightly less formal form of hearing** which usually deal with matters relating to employment law. Their decisions are not always binding on future cases but may be taken into account.

Parliament

Legislation (or **statute law**) is law created by Parliament. There are two main types of legislation: primary and secondary (or delegated) legislation.

International sources of law

A country's laws can also be impacted by sources outside of the country. Very often, countries will make **agreements** with other countries or groups of countries and these agreements may mean that new laws need to be created, or existing laws changed to comply with these agreements.

Types of delegated legislation

- Statutory instruments
- Bye-laws
- Rules of court
- Professional regulations
- Orders in council

Stages in creating legislation

1: First reading
2: Second reading
3: Committee stage
4: Report stage
5: Third reading

Contracts

A **contract** may be defined as an agreement which legally binds the parties, or an agreement which the law will recognise and enforce.

In general, a contract may be **made in any form**. It may be written or oral, or inferred from the conduct of the parties. However, some commercial contracts must be made in writing or in a particular form.

Three essential elements

- Agreement by offer and acceptance
- Intention to create legal relations
- Consideration to be provided by both parties

Other factors affecting the validity of a contract

- **Form**. Some contracts must follow a particular form.
- **Terms**. There may be some implied terms in a contract; express terms may be unlawful.
- **Consent**. There may be misrepresentation inducing one party to enter the contract.
- **Legality**. The courts will not enforce a contract which is illegal or contrary to public policy.
- **Capacity**. Some people have restricted capacity to enter into contracts.

Effect of failure to satisfy the validity tests

- **Void contract**. This is no contract.
- **Voidable contract**. This contract can be avoided by one party.
- **Unenforceable contract**. This contract is valid but performance by one party cannot be forced.

Offer

An **offer** is a **definite promise to be bound on specific terms.** By its nature, it cannot be vague.

Invitation to treat

An invitation to treat is an indication that a person is ready to accept offers with a view to a contract.

Ways an offer can be terminated

- Rejection (outright, or by counter-offer)
- Lapse of specified or reasonable time limit
- Failure of a condition of the offer
- Death of one of the parties (with exceptions)
- Revocation by the offeror (statement or act)

Acceptance

Acceptance is a positive act by a person to whom an offer has been made. If unconditional, the act creates a binding contract.

Communication of acceptance

Acceptance must be communicated to the offeror or it is not effective.

Consideration

Consideration can be defined as **'the element of value in an agreement'** and, in English law, must be supplied by both parties in order to form a binding contract.

Valid consideration

Valid consideration is executed or executory:

Executed consideration. This takes place at the time, eg payment for goods on delivery.

Executory consideration. This is a promise for an act in the future, ie a promise to pay for goods later.

Past consideration

This is not valid consideration. Past consideration is anything done before a promise is made.

Adequacy and sufficiency of consideration

Consideration need not be adequate. It must be sufficient.

Intention

Where there is no express statement as intention to create legal relations, the courts apply **two rebuttable presumptions**:

1 Social, domestic and family arrangements are not usually intended to be binding.

2 Commercial agreements are usually intended to be legally binding.

Methods of discharging a contract

- Agreement
- Frustration
- Performance
- Breach

Breach of contract

A person is in breach of contract when they, without lawful excuse, fail completely and exactly to perform the contract.

Repudiatory contract

Repudiation occurs where a party indicates (by words or action) that they do not intend to honour their contractual obligations.

Repudiatory breach is referred to as **anticipatory breach** where the party declares their intention not to perform before the date that perfomance is due.

Damages

Damages are a common law remedy and are primarily intended to **restore the party** who has suffered loss to the same position they would have been in **if the contract had never been performed**.

Measure of damages

The measure of damages can be to cover the:

Expectation interest (to put the claimant into the position that they would have been in had the contract been performed).

Reliance interest (to compensate the claimant for wasted expenditure caused by their reliance on the contract).

The injured party is expected to **mitigate** their loss as far as reasonably possible.

1: Principles of contract law

Equitable remedies

Specific performance

An order of the court directing a person to perform their contractual obligations → Specific performance will be ordered in instances such as the sale of land. It is **never ordered for personal services** such as in an employment contract.

Injunction

A discretionary court order, requiring a party to observe a negative restriction in a contract → This can be used to enforce restraints in contracts for personal services, for example not working for others.

Rescission

This is the right to rescind voidable contracts → This is not strictly speaking a remedy for breach of contract. It is the right of an injured party to treat the contract as never having existed.

Business-to-consumer contracts

Consumer Rights Act 2015

The Consumer Rights Act 2015 (TSO, 2015) provides statutory control in respect of consumer contracts and consumer notices (such as signs in car parks). It provides that terms in contracts between a business and a consumer will only be binding on the consumer if they are 'fair'. However, the consumer may still rely on a term (and therefore enforce a contract) which is deemed 'unfair'.

When considering whether a term is 'fair', a number of factors should be considered, such as whether it puts the consumer at a disadvantage, if there were any relevant circumstances when the contract was signed, as well as the nature of the contract itself. The test is whether an average consumer who is reasonably well-informed, observant and circumspect would be aware of the term.

In addition, the Act requires that terms are set out in plain, intelligible language and any relevant terms must be prominent.

Two types of term are exempt from the rule on fairness. These are price and subject matter of the contract. However, the Act states that these terms must be sufficiently transparent and prominent in the contract. If they are not, then their fairness will be considered.

1: Principles of contract law

Notes

2: The external business environment

Topic List

Economic environment

Government and the economy

Competitive environment

Businesses are part of and interact with their environment. Micro-economics (such as the laws of supply and demand) affect a business within its immediate business setting or industry. Macro-economic factors (such as taxation, inflation, interest rates, employment and consumer spending) affect businesses within an entire country. Many of these factors create uncertainty and risk that organisations must deal with to survive.

Some organisations take another step and trade in the global market, buying and selling goods and services around the world. The global market brings a whole new set of uncertainties and risks that must be managed.

Economic environment	Government and the economy	Competitive environment

Micro-economic factors

Demand

Demand is the quantity of a good or service that potential purchasers would buy, or attempt to buy, if the price of the good was at a certain level.

Factors affecting demand

- Price
- Inter-related goods: substitutes and complements
- Income levels: normal, inferior and luxury goods
- Fashion and expectations

Supply

Supply is the quantity of a good that existing suppliers or would-be suppliers would want to produce for the market at a given price.

Factors affecting supply

- Price obtainable for the good
- Prices of other goods
- Costs of making the good
- Changes in technology

The profit motive

The profit motive is the long-term objective of an organisation to make money through business transactions, projects or other endeavours.

Macro-economics

Macro-economics describes the wider economy that all businesses and industries operate in within a particular country.

Macro-economic issues

- Economic growth (more goods and services are produced by the economy and society becomes better off)
- Controlling inflation (see inflation box)
- Achieving full employment (all people who can work have a job)
- Achieving a balance between exports and imports (to enable a stable exchange rate for the country's currency)

Inflation and deflation

Inflation is the name given to an increase in price levels generally. A key impact of inflation is that the value of money will fall (ie £100 will buy you fewer goods in the future than it will today).

The opposite to inflation is deflation, a reduction in price levels generally.

A key impact of deflation is that the value of money will rise (ie £100 will buy you more goods in the future than it will today).

Taxation

Purposes of taxation
- To raise money
- To redistribute wealth
- To control the economy (fiscal policy)
- To encourage and discourage various types of activity

Principles of taxation
- Equity
- Certainty
- Convenience
- Economy
- Fairness
- Transparency

Generally speaking, taxation should also be neutral if possible.

Fiscal policy

Fiscal policy is the use of government spending and tax policies to influence the level of aggregate demand in an economy.

Fiscal policy has direct impacts on consumer spending and employment.

Monetary policy

Monetary policy is the use of money supply, interest rates, exchange rates and credit control to influence demand in an economy.

Monetary policy has direct impacts on interest rates, consumer spending and employment.

Types of tax

Revenue taxes

Taxes charged on income (eg salaries or company profit)

Capital taxes

Taxes charged on capital gains or on wealth (eg sale of assets or a deceased person's estate)

Direct taxes

Taxes charged on income, gains and wealth. Direct taxes are collected directly from the taxpayer

Indirect taxes

Taxes paid by the consumer to the supplier who then passes the tax to the government

Global business environment

Businesses do not operate in isolation. They are part of an industry within their home country and, even if they do not trade overseas, are part of the wider global business environment.

Exchange rates

Exchange rates describe the price of a country's currency against other currencies by showing how much of a particular currency one unit of the home currency will buy. For example, £1 might buy £1.20 or $1.40. Another way of looking at it would be that £1 might buy £0.83 or $1 might buy £0.71.

Uncertainty and risk

Uncertainty is created where a business cannot measure or foresee an event or situation occurring.

Risk is the chance of an event occurring that causes loss or damage to a business.

Impacts of exchange rates on business

Value of home currency increases	Value of home currency falls	Risks and uncertainties of trading globally
■ Importers – costs of imported goods and materials fall ■ Exporters – sales may fall as goods sold become more expensive to overseas customers	■ Importers – costs of imported goods and materials rise ■ Exporters – sales may rise as goods sold become cheaper to overseas customers	■ Exchange rate risk ■ Shipping risk ■ Credit risk ■ Global economy ■ International laws and agreements ■ Lack of knowledge

Benefits and disadvantages of trading globally

Benefits	Disadvantages
■ Lower costs	■ Increased competition
■ Larger market	■ Operational issues
■ Risk management	■ Greater overall risk
■ Government incentives	■ Increased costs
■ Access to resources	■ Cultural issues

3: Principles of corporate social responsibility (CSR), ethics and sustainability

Topic List

Social and ethical responsibilities of a business

Sustainability and the environment

Fundamental principles of ethics for accounting technicians

The need to act ethically

In this chapter, we look at how ethical values fit into the role of the finance professional. We also discuss how individuals and organisations have a responsibility to act in a sustainable manner.

Corporate social responsibility (CSR)

CSR is concerned with **business activities** and their impact on **society** and the **environment**.

- Ideally, business activities will benefit both of these areas.
- All individuals working within an organisation have a duty to take responsibility for their actions and to act in a manner consistent with CSR principles.
- Organisations should truly embody CSR principles rather than adopting them just to improve the public's perception of the business.

Business ethics

The concept of **business ethics** suggests that businesses are morally responsible for their actions and should be held accountable for the effects of their actions on people and society.

Stakeholders

(a) **Internal:**

   Corporate management
   Employees

(b) **Connected:**

   Shareholders
   Debt holders (eg bank)
   Intermediate (business) and final (consumer) customers
   Suppliers

(c) **External:**

   Immediate community/society at large
   Competitors
   Special interest groups
   Government

Sustainability

According to the UN's Brundtland Report (1987), **sustainability** means that organisations must aim to "meet the needs of the present without compromising the ability of future generations to meet their own needs".

There are **three aspects** to sustainability:

- Economic sustainability
- Social sustainability
- Environmental sustainability

These aspects link into the **triple bottom line** approach to reporting. This approach can also be summarised as **profit**, **people** and **planet**.

Duties of finance professionals

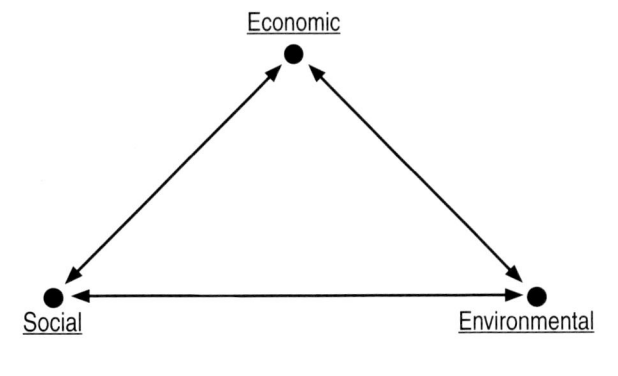

There may be **costs** as well as **benefits** of a business pursuing a sustainable solution. A business will need to weigh up any additional costs and compare them with the benefits received.

Environmental perspectives	Organisational perspectives
Environmental areas of focus include the actions an organisation or those within the accounting function can take in respect of: ■ Environmental care ■ Recycling ■ Energy and resource consumption ■ Travel efficiencies	Organisational areas of focus include the actions an organisation takes in respect of: ■ Its shareholders ■ The acquisition and retention of customers ■ The acquisition and retention of suppliers ■ Delivery of high-quality goods and services ■ Development of employees

3: Principles of corporate social responsibility (CSR), ethics and sustainability

Ethics and ethical values

Ethics are a set of moral principles that guide behaviour.

Ethical values are assumptions and beliefs about what constitutes 'right' and 'wrong' behaviour.

There are five **fundamental principles** set out in the AAT *Code* that underpin ethical behaviour in an accounting context:

Fundamental principle	Explanation
Integrity	A member shall be 'straightforward and honest in all professional and business relationships'.
Objectivity	A member shall 'not allow bias, conflict of interest or undue influence of others to override professional or business judgements'.

Fundamental principle	Explanation
Professional competence and due care	A member has a continuing duty "to maintain professional knowledge and skill at the level required to ensure that a client or employer receives competent professional service based on current developments in practice, legislation and techniques. A member shall act diligently and in accordance with applicable and professional standards when providing professional services".
Confidentiality	A member shall, "in accordance with the law, respect the confidentiality of information acquired as a result of professional and business relationships and not disclose any such information to third parties without proper and specific authority, unless there is a legal or professional right or duty to disclose. Confidential information acquired as a result of professional and business relationships shall not be used for the personal advantage of the member or third parties".
Professional behaviour	A member shall "comply with relevant laws and regulations and avoid any conduct that discredits the profession".

(AAT *Code*, 2017, para. 100.5)

T
H
R
E
A
T
S

- Self-interest
- Self-review
- Advocacy
- Familiarity
- Intimidation

Importance of independence

Independence promotes:

- Reliability of financial information
- Credibility of financial information
- Value for money of audit
- Credibility of profession

Professional safeguards

- Entry requirements
- Training requirements
- CPD requirements
- Professional standards
- Professional monitoring
- Disciplinary procedures
- External review

Safeguards in practice

- Peer review
- Independent consultation
- Partner/staff rotation
- Discussion/disclosure to audit committee
- Reperformance by another firm

Employment with assurance client

Close business relationships

Partner on client board

Financial interest

Family and personal relationships

Recruitment — **SELF-INTEREST THREAT** — Gifts and hospitality

Lowballing

Loans and gurantees

High % of fees

Overdue fees

% or contingent fees

Advocacy threat

An accountant promotes a position or opinion regarding a client to the point that subsequent objectivity may be compromised. Examples include provision of legal service and corporate finance advice.

Conflicts of interest

These can arise from accountants acting for clients with whom they are in dispute, eg over quality of work. It can also arise through disputes between two clients for whom accountants are acting.

Familiarity threat

- Family relationships between client and firm
- Personal relationships between client and firm
- Long association with client
- Recent service with client
- Future employment with client

Intimidation threat

- Close business relationships
- Family relationships
- Personal relationships
- Staff employment by client
- Litigation

3: Principles of corporate social responsibility (CSR), ethics and sustainability

Why behave ethically?

Behaviour in society is regulated by the law, rules and regulations, and in some cases by ethical codes.

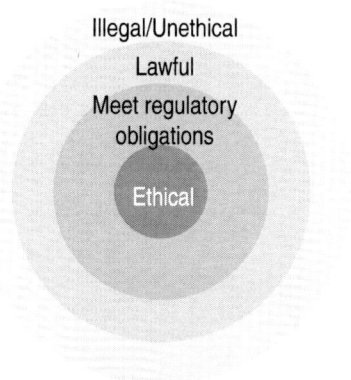

Why should accountants behave ethically?

- Laws and regulation
- Upholding of professional standards and qualities (personal/professional)
- Protection of the public interest
- Avoid disciplinary action by professional body and employer
- Protect employer from fines and reputational damage

Moving from the outside circle inwards, the diagram shows how the actions of an individual can be classed from the least legal/ethical, to being ethical.

Ethical actions

Specific ethical actions

Specific actions that accounting technicians can take to behave ethically include:

- Avoid even the appearance of a conflict of interest
- Be objective and act in the public interest
- Keep sensitive information confidential
- Be straightforward and honest in all dealings
- Maintain professional knowledge, behaviour and skills
- Act within the spirit as well as the letter of the law

3: Principles of corporate social responsibility (CSR), ethics and sustainability

Notes

4: Business entities

Sole traders and partnerships are common forms of business organisation and are commonly used for small businesses and some professional businesses. Unlike sole traders and partnerships, companies are separate legal entities. The key difference between them is the concept of limited liability for the owners.

We will look at several important aspects of sole traders and partnerships before focussing on companies. Here, we shall look at the procedural aspects of company formation and the liability of promoters for pre-incorporation contracts.

This chapter also considers the concept of the public accountability of limited companies in terms of the records they must keep and returns they must make.

Topic List

Models of business ownership

Sole traders

Partnerships

Companies

Entity concept

The entity concept is the principle that some business types have their own identity in law. This means that the business is the true legal owner of its assets and is the only party liable for repaying its debts.

Separation of control and management

The fact that an entity has its own identity in law which is separate from its owners means that there can also be a separation of the owners of the business (who control it) from those that manage it.

Limited liability

Limited liability is a protection offered to owners of certain types of business. This means, in the event of business failure, the owners will only be asked to contribute identifiable amounts to the assets of the business.

Sole traders

Sole traders own and run businesses which are not legally distinct from the owner.

> **Legal status of sole traders**
>
> - No formality
> - Independence and self-accountability
> - Personal supervision
> - All profits accrue to owner
> - Owner's wealth at risk

Taxation

Sole traders are liable to pay income tax and national insurance contributions based on the profits they have earned during each tax year. They may also have to pay VAT and PAYE.

| Models of business ownership | Sole traders | **Partnerships** | Companies |

Partnerships

Partnerships can be very informal – in essence they are **formed when the parties agree** to act in business together.

However, they can be put into place more formally with written **partnership agreements,** and the adoption of **firm name.**

Taxation

Partners are liable to pay income tax and national insurance contributions based on their share of the partnership's profits earned during each tax year. They may also have to pay VAT and PAYE.

Limited Liability Partnership Act 2000 (TSO, 2000)

An 'LLP' is a cross between a company and a partnerships. Crucially, partners have limited liability, so LLPs are more regulated than partnerships.

To be incorporated, the subcribers to the LLP must file the following details with the Registar of Companies:

- The **name** of the LLP
- The **location** of its registered office (in England and Wales, or in Wales, or in Scotland) and its address
- The **names and addresses** of all LLP members
- Who the **designated members** are (who take responsibility for the LLP's publicity requirements)

With regard to publicity, the LLP's designated members must:

- **File** certain notices with the Registar
- Sign and file **accounts**
- Appoint **auditors**, if appropriate

Models of business ownership | Sole traders | Partnerships | **Companies**

Companies

Companies are legal entities, separate from the natural persons connected with them, for example, their members.

Companies own their own assets and are liable for their own debts.

Type of company

Limited
■ Can be limited by shares/guarantee
■ Members' liability limited only (not company's)
■ Two types: private and public

Public
■ May offer securities to the public
■ Name must end with 'plc'
■ Must have a trading certificate to trade

Private
■ May not offer securities to the public
■ Name must end with word 'Limited/Ltd'

Unlimited
■ Members have unlimited liability
■ Can only ever be a private company

Pre-incorporation expenses

Pre-incorporation expenses cannot automatically be recovered by a promoter but, once formed, the company may agree reimbursement.

A pre-incorporation contract

A pre-incorporation contract is a contract purported to be made by a company at a time **before the company has received its certificate of incorporation.**

Liabilities of promoters

The company is **not bound** by pre-incorporation contracts.

Promoters are personally liable on pre-incorporation contracts.

A company is formed when the Registar issues it a **certificate of incorporation**.

To obtain a certificate of incorporation, the promoters of company send the Registrar:

Memorandum of association	The memorandum should be signed by the subscribers. Each subscriber agrees to become a member and to a subscribe for at least one share.
Articles of association (if not default model articles)	Articles are signed by the same subscriber(s), dated and witnessed. Default model articles, relevant to the type of company formed, become the company's articles if no articles are sent to the Registar.
Statement of proposed officers	The statement gives the particulars of the first director(s) and secretary (if applicable). They must consent to act in this capacity.
Statement of compliance	This statement confirms that the requirements of the Companies Act in respect of registration have been complied with.
Statement of capital	A Statement of Capital and Initial Shareholdings must be completed by all companies to be limited by shares.
Registration fee	A registration fee is payable on application.

Statutory rules on company names

- Must end in Ltd (limited) or plc (public limited company) where relevant.
- May not have the same name as another company on the register.
- May not be 'offensive', 'sensitive' or criminal.
- Official approval is required for some words, for example, which suggest an official connection.

Passing off

A company which believes its rights have been infringed may apply for an injuction to restrain another from using a name.

A company can also **appeal to the Company Name Adjudicators** under the Companies Act 2006.

Off-the-shelf companies

The alternative way of setting up a company is to buy a company which has already been registered. This is called buying a company 'off the shelf'.

Advantages	Disadvantages

☑ The application and the following documents are already filed:
   – Memo and articles – Fee
   – Statements of proposed officers, compliance and capital
 ☑ No risk of liability arising on pre-incorporation contracts
	☒ Directors may want to amend the articles (usually default model articles provided)
	 ☒ May need to change the name
	 ☒ Need to transfer subscriber shares

Commencement of business

A **private company** may commence business from the date of incorporation as stated on the certificate of incorporation.

A **public company** must obtain a trading certificate from the Registrar before it is allowed to trade.

Companies

The key source of information on a UK company is its file at **Companies' House**

Companies are also required by law to keep a number of **registers, records** and **returns.**

They must be kept at the company's **registered office** or another registered place know as a **single alternative inspection location (SAIL).**

Statutory registers

Register
Register of members
Register of people with significant control (PSC)
Register of directors and secretaries
Register of directors' residential addresses
Register of directors' services contracts and indemnities
Register of resolutions and meetings of the company
Register of debentureholders
Register of disclosed interests in shares (public company ONLY)

The register of **directors' residential addresses** is not available to the public.

In the register, a director may provide a **service address** instead of their residential address.

Annual accounts

The directors must for each accounting period:

- Prepare a balance sheet and profit and loss account giving a true and fair view
- Lay those accounts and a directors' report before the general meeting of shareholders (public companies only)
- Deliver a copy of those accounts (often in abbreviate form) to the Registrar to be put on the company's file

Accounting records

The directors are required to keep accounting records which show the company's financial position at any given time. They should include:

- Daily entries of sums paid and received
- A record of assets and liabilities
- Statements of stock held at the end of each financial year
- Statements of stocktaking to back up the above
- Statements of goods bought and sold (except retail sales)

Confirmation statement

The company must send a return to the Registrar annually confirming details of, for example, directors, secretary and shares.

Taxation

Companies are required to pay corporation tax on profits earned in each accounting period.

As with the other types of business, companies may also have to register and account for VAT, and pay income tax and national insurance contributions on behalf of their employees through the PAYE system.

5: The finance function

Topic List

Functions of a business

Role of the finance function

Finance function and the success of the organisation

Clearly defining business functions, as well as policies and procedures to follow, are some of the most important factors in creating a successful business. The finance function has a very important role to play in ensuring not only business survival, but effective and efficient operations that help make the business profitable. Communication between all business functions is also critical to make the business successful.

Functions

Organisations look at the various business activities that need to be performed and allocate them to groups known as functions.

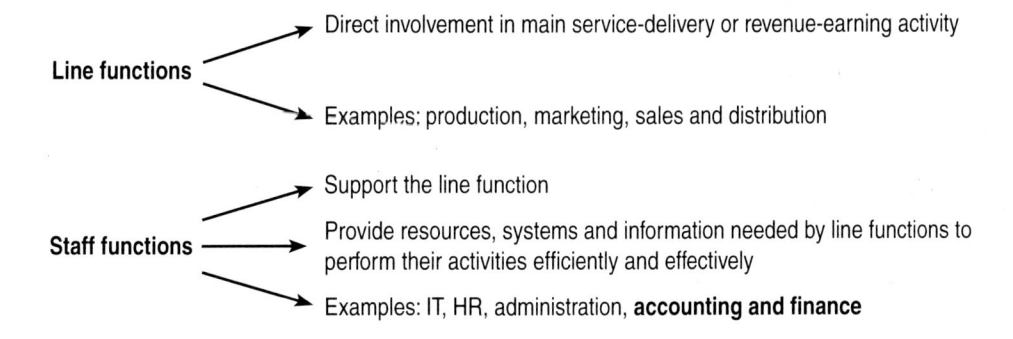

Line functions
→ Direct involvement in main service-delivery or revenue-earning activity

→ Examples: production, marketing, sales and distribution

Staff functions
→ Support the line function

→ Provide resources, systems and information needed by line functions to perform their activities efficiently and effectively

→ Examples: IT, HR, administration, **accounting and finance**

Function	Role
Operations (production)	Plans, organises, directs and controls the necessary activities to provide products and services, creating outputs which have added value over the value of inputs
Sales and marketing	Identifies what customers want and makes sure that the products or services that the business provide meet those needs in a profitable way
Finance	The finance function has four primary roles: 1 Raising money through debt or sale of shares 2 Recording and controlling what happens to the money 3 Providing information to managers 4 Reporting to shareholders and others
Human resources	Involved in recruiting, training, developing and rewarding the organisation's employees
Information technology	Responsible for much of the organisation's infrastructure (eg, computer systems, data storage, software installations, networking and communications)
Distribution and logistics	Responsible for the movement of raw materials and finished goods from where they are to where they need to be

The finance function

Business accounting is the process of:

- Recording all financial transactions carried out by an organisation
- Summarising the transactions to present a financial picture which supports both:
  - Accountability to investors and other external interested parties (or stakeholders); and
  - Internal management decision-making about the business.

This function is often split into other sub-functions.

The data used to prepare management accounts and financial accounts is the same.
The differences between these accounts arise because the data is analysed in a different way.

Management accounts	Financial accounts
■ Distributed internally for use within the business	■ Used for external reporting
■ Management decide on the way in which they are presented	■ Legal requirement for limited companies to prepare them
■ Help management in planning, control and decision making	■ Look at past data only
■ Look at both past and future data	■ Usually include financial information only
■ Not legally required to prepare them	■ Detailed results for a defined period
■ Include both financial and non-financial information	

Payroll is concerned solely with payroll processing eg calculation of gross pay and deductions; preparing payslips; making returns to external agencies (such as HMRC, pension providers); paying employees; preparing payroll statistics.

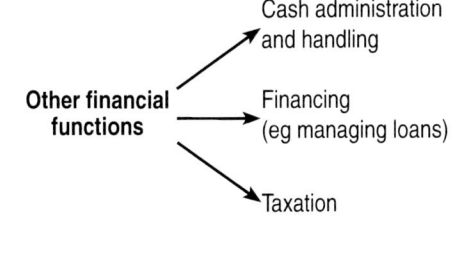

Other financial functions

- Cash administration and handling
- Financing (eg managing loans)
- Taxation

Financial functions are **service and support** providers. Their main role is to provide complete, accurate and timely information on the financial implications of the functions:

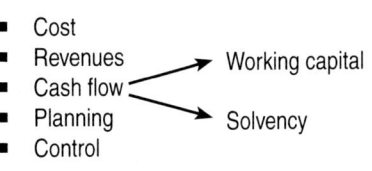

- Cost
- Revenues
- Cash flow → Working capital
- Planning → Solvency
- Control

Outsourcing

Some roles such as payroll may be outsourced. Outsourcing a business process involves finding an outsource partner to provide the service and then drawing up a contract containing the terms of the arrangement such as the service to be provided and the fee to be paid.

Principles of effective communication

In order to be of maximum benefit to the organisation, the information provided by the finance function must be complete, accurate, timely and concise:

Principle	Explanation
Complete	Includes all data relevant to the purpose for which the information will be used
Accurate	Factually and numerically correct, and to an appropriate level of detail for the purpose for which the information will be used
Timely	Delivered at the right time for the information to be meaningful and used to support decision making and action
Concise	Not being overly long in length, being explained precisely but in short, clear language so it is quickly read and understood

The information must also meet the needs of the recipient (can it be used easily for the purpose it is needed for?) and be in an appropriate form or medium (is the information best provided in an email or a formal report?)

Accounting and financial functions make an important contribution in these key areas:

- **Supporting efficient working practices** – achieving objectives with the minimum use of resources eg budgeting and long-term plans used as benchmarks; actual performance details to compare to budget; identify areas where performance and efficiency can be improved.

- **Solvency and long-term financial stability** – managing working capital used in the day-to-day running of the businesss eg provides information on cash flow (cash in and out of the business); planning for cash shortages by obtaining finance; ensures the business is solvent (ie able to pay its debts).

- **Legal and regulatory compliance of the business** – to be able to comply with legislation so that the business benefits from a positive reputation for compliance and so avoid or minimise legal penalties (such as fines).

Compliance with the law is important because:

- The law is there to protect people from loss and suffering, and ensure minimum acceptable standards of management.
- There may be financial penalties (eg fines, compensation) and operational penalties (eg loss of licence) for non-compliance.
- Non-compliance can damage the reputation of the organisation and its ability to attract investors, customers and staff.
- Non-compliance can lead to burdens and costs of corrective action, closer scrutiny in the future and so on.

Policies and procedures

Policies and procedures are set in accordance with the laws and regulations that apply to the organisation. Therefore, if employees follow policies and procedures, the business will comply with the law and regulations.

Policy

is a statement of how an organisation works and expects activities to be carried out.

Examples

Equal opportunities policy; health and safety policy; working hours policy; clear desk policy; confidentiality of information policy; data security policy

Procedure

is a standard sequence of steps or operations necessary to perform an activity.

Examples

Handling of cash receipts; authorisation of payments; secure storage data; timesheets; keeping information confidential and not releasing it to unauthorised persons

Function-specific policies and procedures: These are policies and procedures that apply to specific parts of the business only, for example the finance function.

Organisation-wide policies and procedures: These are policies and procedures that apply to everyone within the organisation, for example HR policies and procedures.

CSR Reporting

Many businesses now provide **sustainability reports**, which detail how sustainable the business model is. Finance professionals have a key role to play in the preparation of such reports.

Integrated reporting is a new approach to corporate reporting, which aims to provide a holistic view of the performance of an organisation by looking not only at financial performance, but on the impact the business has on nature and society as a whole.

6: Working effectively

Topic List

Sources of information

Communicating information

Methods of business communication

Effective written communications

Planning workloads

Meeting deadlines

This chapter covers important skills that are required to be an effective employee in the workplace. We will look at sources of information and various methods of communicating it, such as emails, memos, and brief reports. We also cover the importance of presenting information in the correct, and most appropriate format for users. We will also look at various techniques that can be used to help prioritise tasks and meet set deadlines.

Primary and secondary information

Information may be **primary** (collected specifically for a particular purpose) or **secondary** (collected for some other purpose).

Advantages of primary information	Disadvantages of primary information
The investigator knows where the information has come from	Cost – it can be very expensive to collect primary information
The investigator is aware of any inadequacies or limitations in the information	Time – it can be very time consuming to collect the information

Advantages of secondary information	Disadvantages of secondary information
They are cheaply available.	There may be inadequacies or limitations of the information.
There is potentially a large quantity available.	The information may be out of date.
It is usually quicker to obtain secondary information than primary information.	There may be no relevant information available.
Secondary information can be useful for analysing the past, eg patterns.	The information may be incorrect (especially if found on the internet).

Valid and invalid information

Valid information is relevant, strongly associated and appropriate to the purpose it is being used for.

Invalid information is the direct opposite of valid information. It is not relevant or strongly associated with the purpose it is being put to and therefore it is not appropriate to use it.

Internal and external sources of information

Internal sources of information	External sources of information
Accounting records and reports	Government statistics
Payroll system	Trade journals
Production records	Credit reference agencies
Time sheets	Marketing agencies
Customer account records	The internet

There are several benefits of using information from more than one source.

Benefits
■ One source may corroborate information from another source, increasing the overall reliability of the information
■ Reduces the risk that information might be biased, as bias in one information source may be compensated by the other information source
■ Provides a wider perspective of the overall picture created by the information
■ Accuracy of information from one source can be confirmed by another source
■ Having multiple sources of information should make it easier to find valid information

Recognising sources of information

Importance of recognising information sources

It allows the reader to refer back to the original source documents for more information or to verify your information.

It helps the reader decide whether your information is valid, accurate and reliable for their purposes.

It demonstrates professional standards and presentation of your work.

If the information is being published outside of the organisation, then references are required to comply with rules on copyright.

| Sources of information | Communicating information | Methods of business communication | Effective written communications | Planning workloads | Meeting deadlines |

Working effectively in finance is fundamentally about the effective preparation, giving and receiving of information. All of this requires effective comminication – with colleagues, with other departments and with stakeholders outside the organisation.

Information communicated should be:

- Complete
- Accurate
- Timely
- Fit for purpose

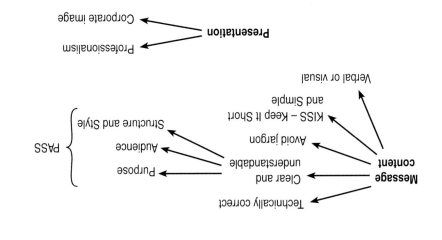

Business letters

A letter is a very flexible and versatile medium of written, person-to-person communication. It can be used for many business purposes: requesting, supplying and confirming information and instructions; offering and accepting goods and services; conveying and acknowledging satisfaction and dissatisfaction.

Emails

Email is a method for sending electronic messages from one computer to another, either internally within the workplace or to an external party. Email is easy to use, extremely fast and relatively cheap. It is also particularly flexible, because photos, diagrams, computer files and/or spreadsheets can be sent (with the email as a kind of 'covering letter') as attachments.

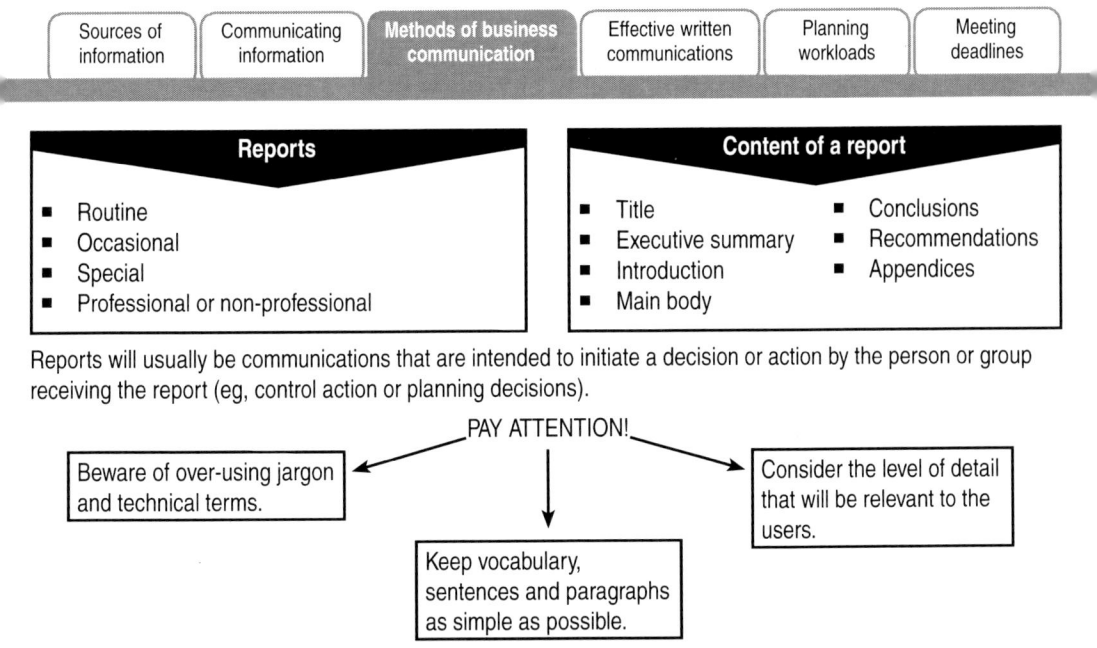

Reports	**Content of a report**
■ Routine ■ Occasional ■ Special ■ Professional or non-professional	■ Title ■ Conclusions ■ Executive summary ■ Recommendations ■ Introduction ■ Appendices ■ Main body

Reports will usually be communications that are intended to initiate a decision or action by the person or group receiving the report (eg, control action or planning decisions).

PAY ATTENTION!

Beware of over-using jargon and technical terms.

Keep vocabulary, sentences and paragraphs as simple as possible.

Consider the level of detail that will be relevant to the users.

Spreadsheets

A spreadsheet is essentially an electronic piece of paper divided into rows and columns with a built-in pencil, eraser and calculator. It provides an easy way of performing numerical calculations and presenting information.

Social media communications

The success of social networking sites such as Twitter and Facebook has resulted in many businesses and individuals having somewhere where they can share information with others.

Social media allows users and organisations to interact in several ways:

- Posting a status update containing information about what the user has been doing, or thoughts they have on particular issues
- Sharing media such as photos, music and videos
- Sharing links to websites and news reports
- Sharing posts containing all the above that other users have made
- Sending direct messages privately to other users

Impacts of inappropriate sharing of information and social media communications

Impacts
■ Loss of confidential information ■ System damage ■ Identity theft ■ Deliberate damage to reputation ■ Damage to reputation due to negligent or inappropriate behaviour

Intranet

An intranet is used to disseminate and exchange information 'in-house' within an organisation. The idea behind an intranet is that companies set up their own mini version of the internet. Each employee has a browser, used to access a server computer that holds corporate information on a wide variety of topics, and in some cases also offers access to the internet.

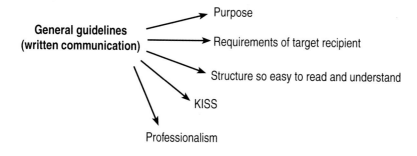

General guidelines (written communication)
- → Purpose
- → Requirements of target recipient
- → Structure so easy to read and understand
- → KISS
- → Professionalism

Salutation	Close	Context
Dear Sir/Madam/Sirs (name not used)	Yours faithfully	Formal situations Recipients not known
Dear Dr/Mr/Mrs/Ms Bloggs (formal name used)	Yours sincerely	Established relationships Friendly but respectful (eg with superiors, customers, suppliers)
Dear Joe/Josephine	Yours sincerely Kind regards	More personal, informal relationships (eg with colleagues)

Business Letters

Content of business letters

- The name and address of the target recipient
- The address of the sender
- Date
- Greeting (or 'salutation')
- Subject heading (a brief, helpful 'cue' to what the letter is about)
- An opening paragraph

- The main body of the letter
- A closing paragraph
- Sign-off (or 'complimentary close')
- Signature
- Enclosure reference
- Copy reference

Email template

```
To:        [Recipient's email address: name@company.co.uk or similar]
Cc:        [Email addresses of parties to whom the message is copied]
From:      [Sender's email address]
Date:      [Today's date]
Subject:   [Concise statement of main theme or topic of message]
Attach:    [Name of file attached to the message]
```

The main text of the email should be written in correct, readily understandable English, in spaced paragraphs following a clear, logical structure and a simple format – avoid the use of **bold**, underlined, *italic* or CAPITALISED text (capitals in an email give an impression of you shouting, which is not professional).

Name/initials (optional)

Signature block (inserted automatically, if used)

Routine tasks

- Open post
- Deal with emails
- Pay suppliers' invoices
- Prepare sales invoices
- Prepare bank reconciliation

Unexpected tasks

- Prepare report for manager
- Cover for sick colleague
- Help colleague to meet a deadline

Priorities

Urgent and important tasks

|

Not urgent but important tasks

|

Urgent but not important tasks

|

Not urgent and not important tasks

Scheduling

If important tasks appear, you must be prepared to change priorities and the order in which tasks are carried out.

Once you have a list of priorities, **schedule** tasks by determining when they will be done.

Meeting deadlines

Deadline
■ If a deadline is unlikely to be met it must be reported immediately. ■ Manager may be able to change deadline/ organise assistance/lighten your existing work load/provide additional resources.

Seeking assistance

- Must recognise that assistance is required
- Identify assistance/resources required
- Negotiate the assistance
- Co-ordinate the assistance

Notes

7: Importance of information

Topic List

Role of information in the finance function

Importance of data and information security

Businesses need information which is useful to make decisions. Information which is produced by the finance function must be useful. Information systems are rapidly developing so it is important to know how systems that accountants use collect, process and disseminate information.

Organisations are required by law to keep data and information they hold safe and secure. There are several methods to achieve this. Cybersecurity is of great importance in reducing the threats from cyber risks.

The finance function and information

The finance function supports the other business functions in fulfilling their objectives and, through them, the overall objectives of the organisation.

Information received by the finance function	Examples
Budgetary	Staff numbers Production information Marketing costs Planned investments in equipment
Inventory control and costing information	Stock valuations Inventory counts Hourly wage rates Overheads

Information received by the finance function	Examples
Information from suppliers and customers	Information received to set-up and manage supplier and customer accounts such as: Name, address, phone number and email address Credit reports obtained concerning customers Financial statements sent in by customers Contracts with suppliers
Purchase orders	Requests by individual departments to purchase materials
Remittance advice	Confirmation from suppliers that they have been paid
Statements	Records of supplier accounts that show invoices, payments and credit notes
Supplier invoices	Invoices for each order placed with a supplier
Credit notes	Records of credit notes issued by suppliers

Information produced by the finance function	Examples
Information to help management decision making	Management accounts Variance reports Costing information
Budgetary information	Budgets for each department Master budget for the whole organisation
Cash information	Details of cash at bank Fixed term investments and when they are due to mature Forecasted cash receipts and payments
Taxation information	VAT payable/refunds due Corporation tax PAYE/NIC contributions on employee salaries

Information produced by the finance function	Examples
Information for suppliers and customers	Information given to suppliers and customers to set-up and manage accounts such as: Name, address, phone number and email address Financial statements given to suppliers Contracts with customers
Sales invoices	Details of each order placed by a customer
Credit notes	Records of credit notes issued to customers
Statements	Breakdown of each customer's account (invoices, payments and credit notes)

Characteristics of useful information

Useful information has the following characteristics:

Characteristic	Explanation
Comparable	Information is prepared in a manner which allows it to be accurately compared across time periods and organisational departments. Comparability depends on consistency.
Consistent	Information is prepared using the same methods (policies and calculations) each time.
Understandable	Information is presented in a clear format and in easy-to-read language that allows readers to fully appreciate the information that is being presented.
Relevant and reliable	Only information that is required for a decision is presented. Information that is presented is valid and can be trusted as accurate.
Timely	Information is made available when needed (before or at the time of the decision).

Digital technologies

Modern digital technologies are available to assist the finance function in collection, processing and disseminating financial information. Collectively, they are known as fintech.

Fintech	Explanation
Big data	Describes sets of data of such size that traditional databases are unable to store, manage or analyse them
Data analytics	The collection, management and analysis of large data sets (such as big data) with the objective of discovering useful information, such as customer buying patterns, that an organisation can use for decision making
Distributed ledger technology (Blockchain)	Technology that allows organisations and individuals who are unconnected to share an agreed record of events, such as ownership of an asset

Fintech	Explanation
Cloud computing	Involves the provision of computing as a consumable service instead of a purchased product. It enables system information and software to be accessed by computers remotely as a utility through the internet.
Cloud accounting	The provision of accountancy software through the cloud. Users log in to the accountancy software to process financial transactions and produce management reports in the same way as if the software was installed on their own machine.

Artificial intelligence

The ability of a computer system to assist a human operator to make business decisions or help solve problems

Automation

In the context of Fintech, Automation refers to the ability of systems to perform routine activities and process data without the input of a human.

Privacy and confidentiality

Certain types of information may be designated as confidential by law, regulation, organisational policy and professional Codes of Practice. Organisations that process personal information need to comply with the EU General Data Protection Regulation (GDPR) and the UK's Data Protection Act.

Examples of confidential information

- Details of customers and suppliers
- Personal data about employees
- Financial and other company information

The need to keep information secure

Information held in files, records and computers needs to be protected from accidental or malicious damage, loss, theft, sabotage, interference – and prying eyes. Most organisations have policies and procedures covering data security.

Document retention

- Many accounting and banking records (including ledgers, invoices, cheques, paying-in counterfoils, bank statements and instructions to banks) should be kept for **six years**.
- Employee records (including staff personnel records, time cards and piecework records, payroll records and expenses claims) should also be kept for **six years** – and accident report books, permanently.

Cyber risk, cyber attacks and cyber security

Cyber risk

A number of organisational risks which are possible consequences of a cyber-attack. Cyber risks include: financial losses, reputational damage and operational disruption.

Cyber attacks

Deliberate attempts to damage an organisation by using the internet to take advantage of poor security controls and system integrity

Cyber security

The protection of computer systems from the risk of cyber attack through the use of hardware and software security procedures and controls

Notes

Notes

Notes

Notes